Contents

Can you clap your hands and click your fingers? When you stamp your feet and slap your thighs do you make a sound?

Do you make a noise when you blow through your hands? Can you hum, sing or even whistle?

STARTERS

Musical Instruments

Liz Gogerly

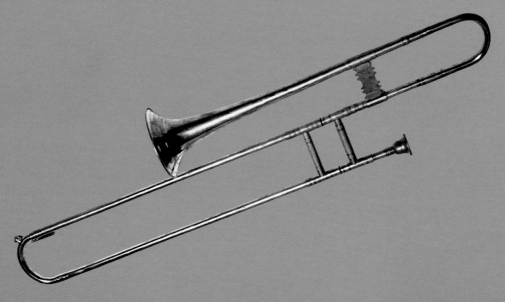

Text copyright © Liz Gogerly 2004

Language consultant: Andrew Burrell
Subject consultant: Deena Day
Design: Perry Tate Design
Picture research: Glass Onion Pictures

Published in Great Britain in 2004
by Hodder Wayland, an imprint of
Hodder Children's Books

This paperback edition published in 2008 by Wayland,
a division of Hachette Children's Books, an Hachette Livre UK company.

The publishers would like to thank the following for allowing us to reproduce their
pictures in this book: Lebrecht Collection; title page, 13 (bottom), 15, 16 (bottom),
18 (top), 22 / Getty Images; contents page, 8 (top), 11 (top), 17 (bottom) / Topham
Picturepoint; 4 (top), 23 / Hodder Wayland Picture Library; cover, 4 (bottom), 6, 8
(bottom), 9 (bottom), 10, 12 (bottom), 14 (top), 16 (top), 18 (bottom) / Corbis; 5, 7, 9
(top), 11 (bottom), 14 (bottom), 17 (top), 20, 21 / Angela Hampton; 12 (top) /
Redferns; 13 (top), 19

A catalogue record for this book is available from the British Library.

ISBN: 978 0 7502 4556 2

Printed and bound in China

Wayland
A division of Hachette Children's Books
338 Euston Road, London NW1 3BH

All you need to make music is your body
and your voice – it's as
easy as that!

With musical instruments we can make lots of other noises and sounds too.

Some instruments like the piano are more difficult to play. You might need lessons.

It looks easy to play a drum. But you do need rhythm.

Whatever instrument you play it can be lots of fun!

Shake, rattle and roll!

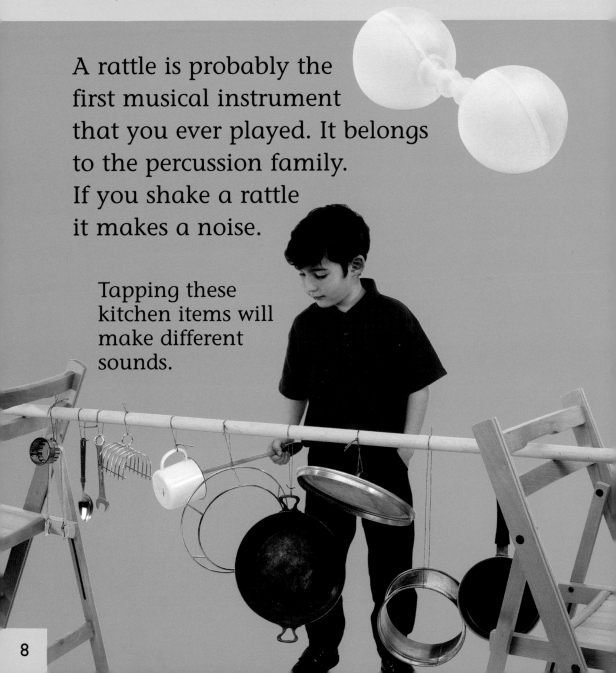

A rattle is probably the first musical instrument that you ever played. It belongs to the percussion family. If you shake a rattle it makes a noise.

Tapping these kitchen items will make different sounds.

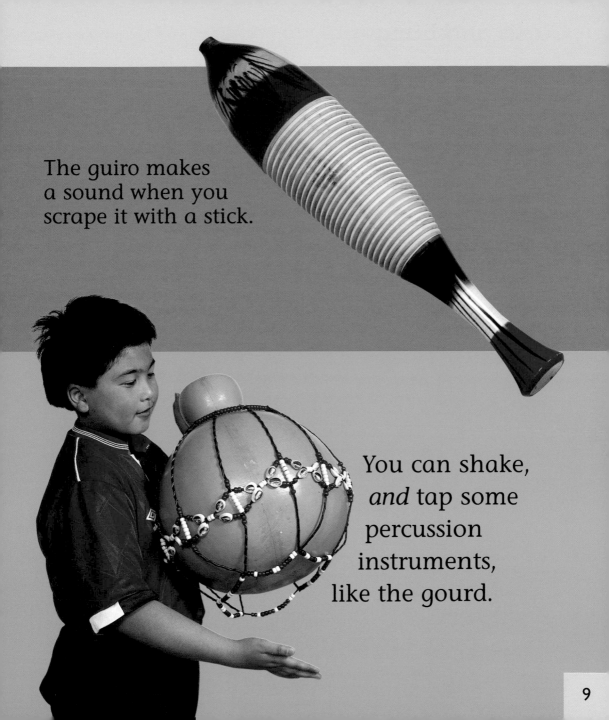

The guiro makes
a sound when you
scrape it with a stick.

You can shake,
and tap some
percussion
instruments,
like the gourd.

Clash and bang

When you **clash** a pair of cymbals together they can be very loud. It sounds like a big wave breaking on the beach.

You can **bang** a drum with a stick. But, if you tap it with your hands it makes a quieter sound.

The marimba is like a xylophone. It is made of wood so it makes a soft sound too.

Playing with strings

Instruments with strings, like the guitar or the violin, are called string instruments.

When each string is plucked you hear a different note.

Some string instruments can be played with a bow. You SLIDE the bow across the strings to make a sound.

A piano is also a
string instrument.
The strings are
hidden inside
its body.

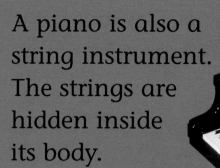

When you press a
key a hammer strikes a
string inside the piano.

strings

hammers

Each key plays
a different note.

keys

Big strings, little strings

Where do different notes come from?

The THIN strings make the high notes.

The strings on a sitar are thin so the sound is high.

And, the **THICK** strings make the low notes.

The strings on the double bass are thick so the sound is lower.

LONG strings sound deeper than SHORT strings too. The concert harp has 47 strings of different length and thickness. That's why the harp has a magical sweeping sound.

One of the biggest string instruments is a harp.

Wind and brass instruments

Wind and brass instruments need you to blow into them to make a sound.

The trumpet makes a cheeky TOOT TOOT sound. You change the notes by pressing the keys.

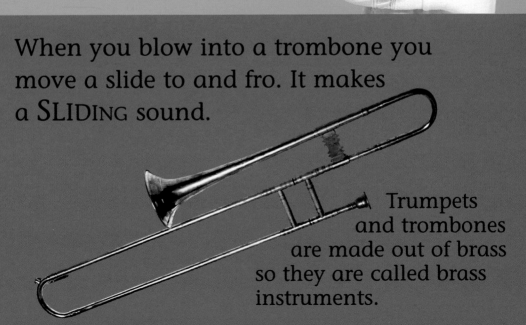

When you blow into a trombone you move a slide to and fro. It makes a SLIDING sound.

Trumpets and trombones are made out of brass so they are called brass instruments.

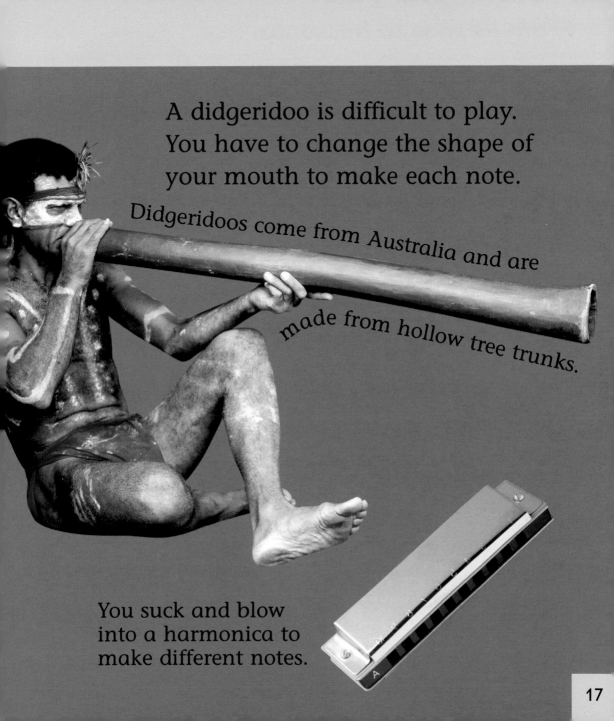

A didgeridoo is difficult to play. You have to change the shape of your mouth to make each note.

Didgeridoos come from Australia and are made from hollow tree trunks.

You suck and blow into a harmonica to make different notes.

It's easy to play a kazoo. It makes a funny sound because you sing into the mouthpiece.

The smallest recorder sounds HIGH like a whistle. The biggest recorder sounds LOW and **smooth**.

18

A bassoon is much bigger than a recorder. It makes a **DEEP** velvety sound like a sleepy hippopotamus.

It's great fun to twang a guitar. An electric guitar is plugged into an amplifier to make it sound **LOUDER**.

Many people in pop bands play electric guitars. They can make lots of exciting sounds.

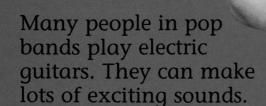

An electric keyboard can sound just the same as a piano. But you can also change the sound or add a rhythm.

A synthesizer is an electronic instrument. You can make hundreds of different noises – from sweet tweets to **DEEP** bleeps.

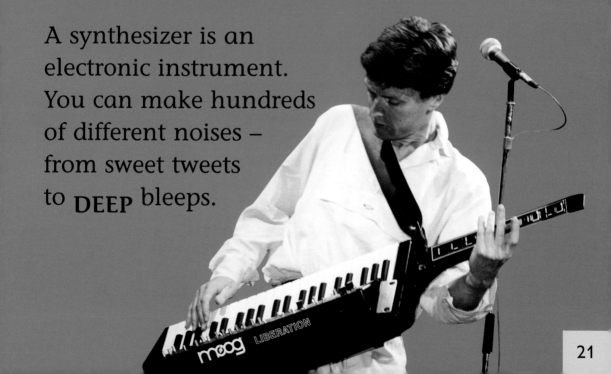

All together now!

Whatever instrument you play it's brilliant to make music with other people.

The music might be beautiful to listen to...

Or good to dance to. And it usually brings a big smile to everybody's face.

Glossary and index

Amplifier An electronic piece of equipment that makes sounds or notes louder. **20**

Electric instruments Instruments that need electricity to make them work. **20, 21**

Keys The buttons that you press on an instrument to play different notes. **13, 16**

Mouthpiece The part of an instrument that is held to the lips and blown into. **18**

Percussion instruments Instruments that are tapped, shaken or scraped to make a sound. **8, 9, 10, 11**

Pluck When the string on an instrument is pulled by your finger then let go to make a sound. **12**

Synthesizer An electronic instrument that can make lots of different sounds when the keys are pressed. **21**

Wind and brass instruments Instruments that are played by breathing air into them. Some are made of brass. **16, 17, 18, 19**